HAND ART

by the editors of KLUTZ®

Make some Hand Art!

1 Place your hand on the paper in the shape you wish to draw.

2 Trace your hand.

3 Color in with crayons.

4

Decorate with googly eyes and pompoms.

TURKEY

Peacock

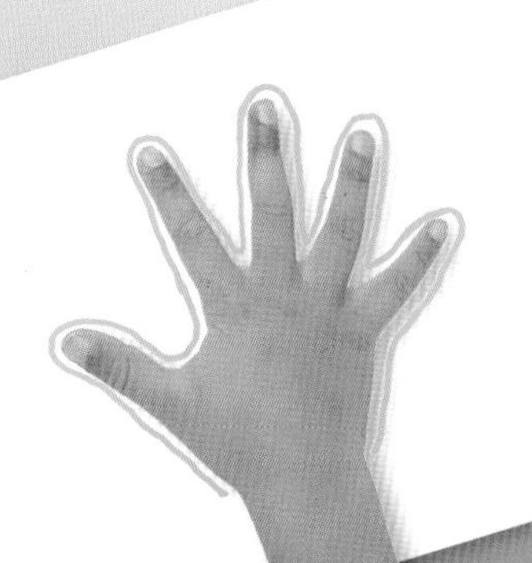

Bunny

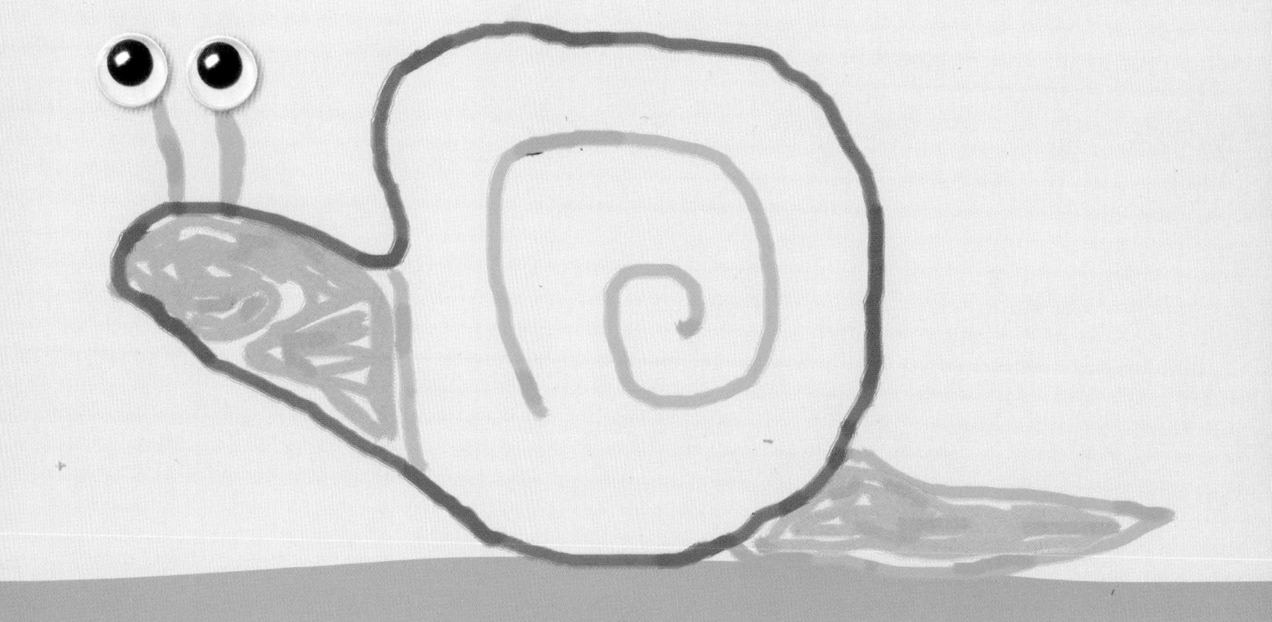

Snail

WOOF!
DOG

Decorate
your fridge
with pages
of fabulous
hand art!

GHOST

BAT

Have someone help you trace your hands. Do not trace your thumbs for the bat!

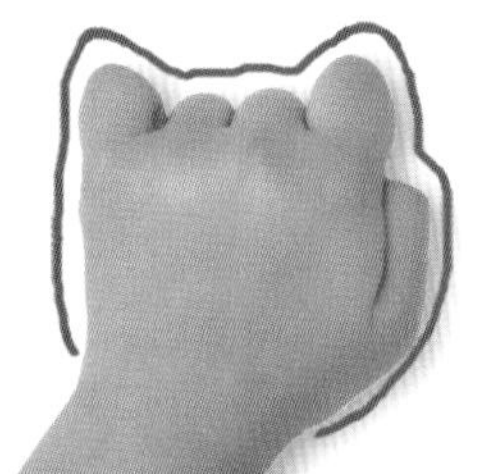

cat

...HORSE

Jellyfish

OCTOPUS
After you trace your hand, turn the page around until the fingers point down.

alien

Sea Monster

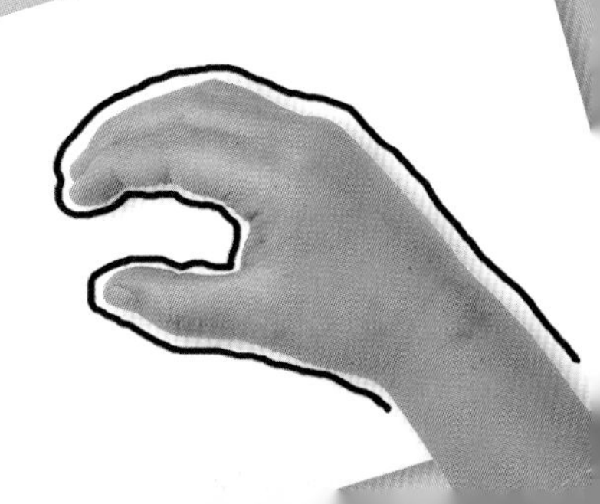

Giraffe

Elephant

After you trace your hand, **turn** the page around until the knuckles point down.

BOO!
Dragon

FROG

Butterfly
RACE CAR RED
Have someone help
you trace your hands!

HANDY PERSON
After you trace your hand, **turn** the page around until the fingers point down.

More Great Chicken  Socks® Books

Make Your Own Twinkly Tiaras • Melty Beads

The Foam Book • **Fun With Felt** • **Highlight This Book!**

Crayon Rubbings • **Magic Painting** • **Totally Tape**

Utterly Elegant Tea Parties • The Super Scissors Book

Pop Bead People • **Shadow Games** • **How to Tell Time**

Can't get enough?
Here are some simple ways to keep the Klutz coming.

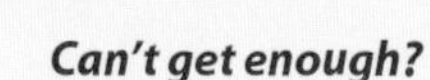

- Order **more of the supplies** that came with this book at Klutz.com. It's quick, it's easy and, seriously, where else are you going to find this exact stuff?
- Get your hands on a copy of **The Klutz Catalog**. To request a free copy of our mail order catalog go to klutz.com/catalog.
- Become a **Klutz Insider** and get e-mail about new releases, special offers, contests, games, goofiness and who-knows-what-all. If you're a grown-up who wants to receive e-mail from Klutz, head to www.klutz.com/socks.

If any of this sounds good to you but you don't feel like going online right now, just give us a call at 1-800-737-4123. We'd love to hear from you.